Team 1 Together

Activity Book

T0386005

Contents

Pearson

Classroom language

1 **Look and match.**

Write.

Read.

Draw.

Listen.

Look.

Point.

2 **Look and circle.**

1 Draw.
  Read.

2 Look.
  Write.

3 Read.
  Listen.

4 Point.
  Draw.

3 **Look and trace.**

1 Open your book.　**2** Wave goodbye.　**3** Sit down.

4 Pick up your book.　**5** Stand up.　**6** Close your book.

4 **Read and tick (✔) or cross (✗).**

1 　Stand up.　☐

2 　Pick up your book.　☐

3 　Wave goodbye.　☐

4 　Close your book.　☐

Hello!

1 **Look and trace.**

Lucy

Marie

Ben

Sam

Einstein

2 (S4) **Listen and number.**

3 **Write, draw and colour.**

Sam   five   six

Hello! I'm <u>Sam</u>. What's your name?

My name's _____.

Hi, _____. I'm seven. How old are you?

I'm _____.

_____

<u>Sam</u>

1 **Trace, match and colour.**

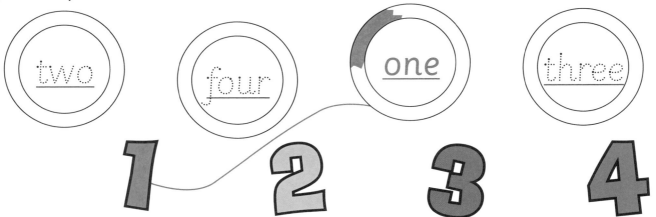

2 **Read, trace and draw.**

1 How many balloons?
<u>Six</u> balloons.

2 How many balloons?
<u>Seven</u> balloons.

3 How many balloons?
<u>Eight</u> balloons.

4 How many balloons?
<u>Nine</u> balloons.

5 How many balloons?
<u>Ten</u> balloons.

1   **Trace and colour.**

1   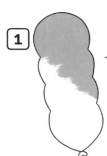   *blue*

2 

orange

pink

3 

black

4 

2   **Read and trace.**

1 What colour is it?

Green. It's *green*.

2 What colour is it?

Brown. It's *brown*.

3 What colour is it?

Blue. It's *blue*.

4 What colour is it?

Purple. It's *purple*.

5 What colour is it?

Red. It's *red*.

1

2

3

4

5

1 Look at my toys!

1 ⏱ **Look at Pupil's Book page 10. Read and circle.**

1 How many balloons can you see?   (six) seven

2 What colour is the teddy?   blue   brown

3 What colour is the plane?   orange   yellow

2 **Look, trace and match.**

 a

 b

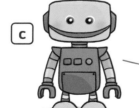 c

d

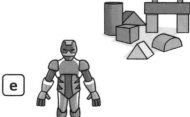 e

1 <u>robot</u>

2 <u>puzzle</u>

3 <u>dinosaur</u>

4 <u>doll</u>

5 <u>teddy</u>

6 <u>yoyo</u>

7 <u>building set</u>

8 <u>plane</u>

9 <u>car</u>

10 <u>action figure</u>

 f

 g

 h

i

 j

3 🎧 **1.5 Listen and tick (✔).**

1   a   b

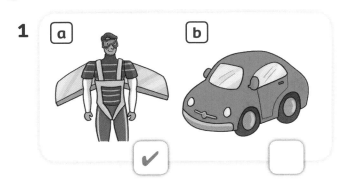

✔

2   a   b

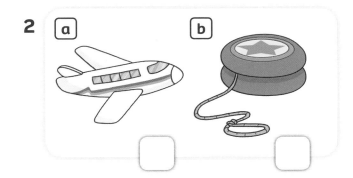

3   a   b

4   a   b

4   **Read and circle.**

1 It's a robot (dinosaur).

2 It's a plane car.

3 It's a building set puzzle.

4 It's a doll teddy.

1 `After you read` **Remember the story. Read and number.**

2 `Values` **Look and tick (✔).**

3 💡 **Look and colour.**

1 **Find and colour. Then trace and match.**

bike   ball   scooter

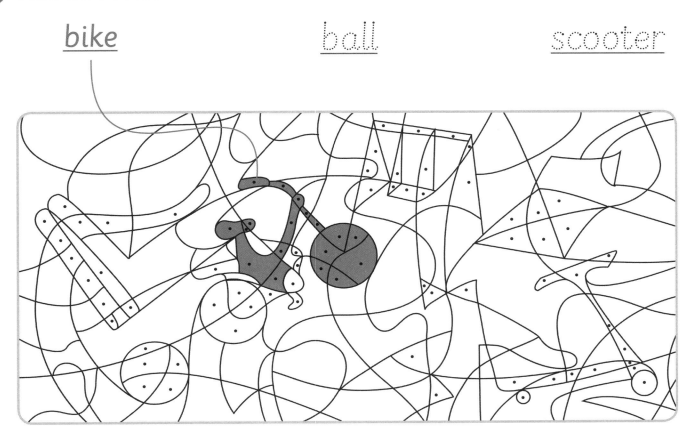

kite   swing   slide

2 **Read and circle.**

1 Is it a ball?

Yes, it is.

No, it isn't.

2 Is it a kite?

Yes, it is.

No, it isn't.

3 Is it a swing?

Yes, it is.

No, it isn't.

4 Is it a slide?

Yes, it is.

No, it isn't.

》》》 Extra practice, page 16

1 **Look, read and write. Then circle.**

~~ball~~ car teddy ~~red~~ robot purple

1 What's this? It's a ___ball___ . It's ___red___ .

2 What's this? It's a _____ . It's _____ .

3 Is it a red _____ ? Yes, it is. No, it isn't.

4 Is it a brown _____ ? Yes, it is. No, it isn't.

2  **Trace, draw a toy and write.**

What's this?

It's a _____ . It's _____ .

CULTURE 1

1 **Read and match.**

jungle gym   museum   board game

1   2   3

2 After you read **Read and circle.**

1

It's a school (museum).

2

It's a toy jungle gym .

3

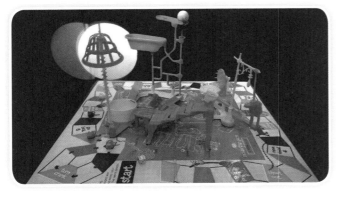

It's a board game slide .

1 **Write, draw and colour. Then act out.**

bike   ball   doll   building set   yoyo

What's this?

It's my new _____.

Can I play with it, please?

Yes, of course.

Great!

My _____

Phonics

2 🎧(1.18) **Listen, trace and match.**

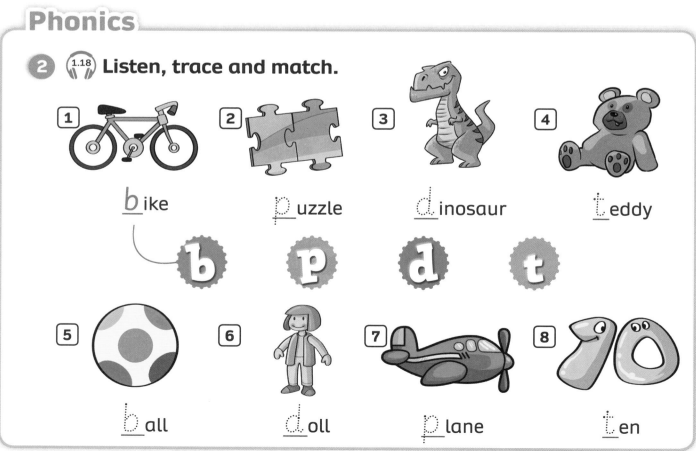

1 b̲ike   2 p̲uzzle   3 d̲inosaur   4 t̲eddy

b   p   d   t

5 b̲all   6 d̲oll   7 p̲lane   8 t̲en

1 **Look and write.**

kite puzzle scooter yoyo

| 1 | 2 | 3 | 4 |

It's a   It's a   It's a   It's a

_____kite_____.   _____.   _____.   _____.

2 **Read and circle.**

1 Is it a slide?   **2** Is it a ball?   **3** Is it a swing?   **4** Is it a puzzle?

(Yes, it is.)   Yes, it is.   Yes, it is.   Yes, it is.

No, it isn't.   No, it isn't.   No, it isn't.   No, it isn't.

3 **Draw your favourite toy. Then write.**

It's _____.

1 Find and colour. Then trace and tick (✔).

☑ <u>puzzle</u>

☐ scooter

☐ teddy

☐ building set

☐ doll

☐ swing

☐ slide

☐ bike

2 Look and trace.

1 What is it? It's a <u>kite</u>.

2 What is it? It's a <u>plane</u>.

3 What is it? It's a <u>ball</u>.

4 What is it? It's a <u>robot</u>.

Get ready for...

Pre A1 Starters Reading and Writing Part 1

1 🎯 **Look and read. Put a tick (✔) or a cross (✗) in the box.**

1

This is a ball.

2

This is a bike.

3

This is a doll.

4

This is a scooter.

5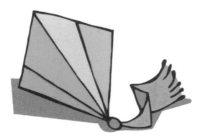

This is a kite.

2 Where's my pen?

1 🕐 **Look at Pupil's Book page 20. Read and circle.**

1 How many cars can you see?   two (eight)

2 What colour is the scooter?   brown   blue

3 How many bikes can you see?   one   two

2 Look, trace and match.

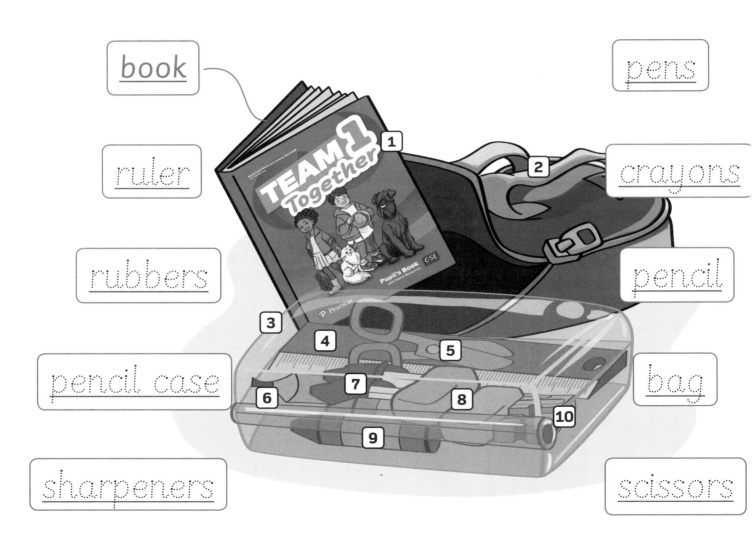

book   pens

ruler   crayons

rubbers   pencil

pencil case   bag

sharpeners   scissors

3 (2.5) **Listen and number.**

a

b

`1`

c

d

4 **Read, match and colour.**

1 (This is my green sharpener.)

2 (This is my yellow bag.)

3 (These are my blue crayons.)

4 (These are my pink rubbers.)

a

b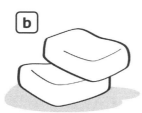

c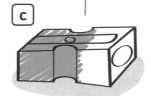

d

1 `After you read` **Remember the story. Read and match.**

1 Oh! It's a computer. It's great.

2 These are my books and this is Atomic, my cat.

3 This is my desk. This is my pen and these are my pencils.

4 Let's tidy up.

2 `Values` **Look and match.**

books

pencils

crayons

sharpeners

pens

rubbers

scissors

3 **Look and colour.**

The computer

1 **Look, trace and number.**

	table
1	shelf
	computer
	cupboard
	desk
	chair

2 **Read and circle.**

1 Where's the ruler?

It's on (under) the chair.

2 Where's the computer?

It's in on the desk.

3 Where's the shelf?

It's in under the cupboard.

4 Where's the chair?

It's on under the table.

5 Where's the book?

It's in on the shelf.

6 Where's the teddy?

It's under in the bag.

>> Extra practice, page 26

1 **Read and tick (✔).**

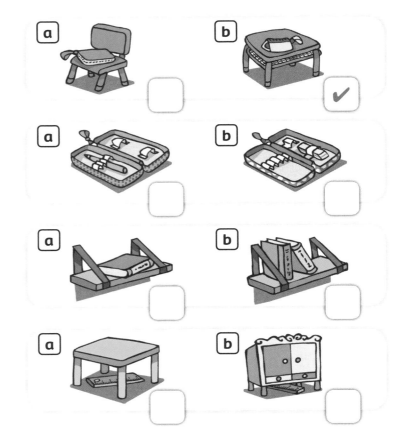

1 This is my pencil case.
It's on the desk.

2 This is my pencil.
It's in my pencil case.

3 This is my book.
It's on the shelf.

4 This is my ruler.
It's under the table.

2 **Choose, draw a teddy and write.**

in   on   under   the table   the desk   the bag

Where's the small teddy? What colour is it?

It's _____. It's _____.

CULTURE · 2

1 **Read and match.**

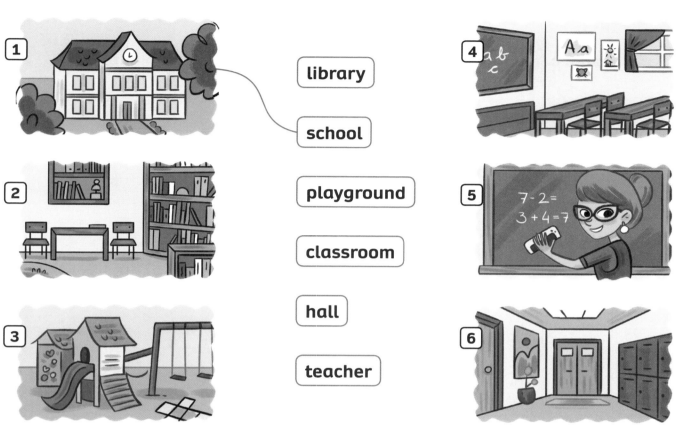

library

school

playground

classroom

hall

teacher

2 After you read **Read and write** Yes **or** No.

1 Is it the computer room? ___No___ **2** Is it the library? _____

3 Is it the classroom? _____ **4** Is it the playground? _____

English in action
Borrowing things

1 **Write, draw and colour. Then act out.**

| sharpener | rubber | ruler | book | crayon |

Is this your _____?

Yes, it is.

Can I borrow it, please?

Yes. Here you are.

Thank you.

My _____

Phonics

2 (2.18) **Listen, trace and match.**

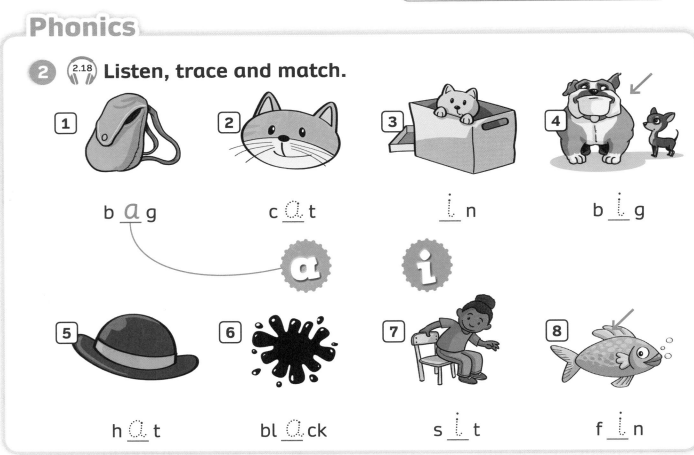

1 b a g

2 c a t

3 i n

4 b i g

a

i

5 h a t

6 bl a ck

7 s i t

8 f i n

1 Look and write.

This   These

1 <u>This</u> is my bag.

2 _____ are my books.

3 _____ are my crayons.

4 _____ is my ruler.

2 Read, circle and write.

table   cupboard   ~~shelf~~   desk

1 Where's the book?   It's **in** (**on**) the _____shelf_____ .

2 Where's the ruler?   It's **in** **on** the _____ .

3 Where's the chair?   It's **on** **under** the _____ .

4 Where's the pen?   It's **under** **on** the _____ .

3 Read and draw.

1 These are my books.

2 This is my pencil case.

1 **Find and colour. Then count.**

a These are
my pens. 3

b This is
my ruler. ☐

c These are
my crayons. ☐

d This is
my book. ☐

e These are
my rubbers. ☐

f This is
my pencil case.  ☐

2 **Look at Activity 1. Read and write.**

in   on   under   cupboard   chair   desk   ~~table~~

1 Where's the computer?   It's _____on_____ the ___table___ .

2 Where's the bag?   It's _____ the _____ .

3 Where's the pencil case?   It's _____ the _____ .

4 Where's the book?   It's _____ the _____ .

Get ready for...

Pre A1 Starters Reading and Writing Part 3

1 Look at the pictures. Look at the letters. Write the words.

1

<u>b o o k</u>

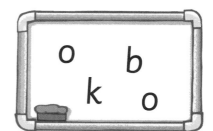

o   b
k   o

2

_ _ _ _ _ _

e   l
c
n   p   i

3

_ _ _ _

e   k
d   s

4

_ _ _ _ _ _

e   r
l
u   r

5

_ _ _ _ _ _ _ _

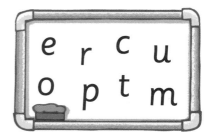

e   r   u
c
o   p   t   m

③ Move your body!

1 🕐 **Look at Pupil's Book page 30. Read and write.**

orange ~~bag~~ four

1 Where's the ruler?   It's in the _bag_.

2 What colour is the swing?   It's O_____.

3 How many bags can you see?   F_____.

2 **Look, trace and match.**

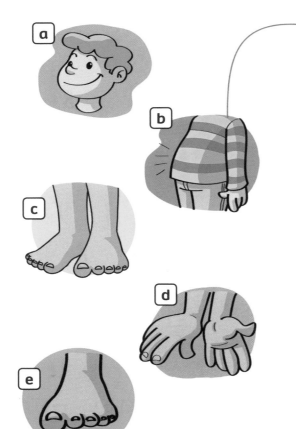

a

b

c

d

e

1 tummy

2 head

3 feet

4 toes

5 hands

6 face

7 arms

8 fingers

9 legs

10 knees

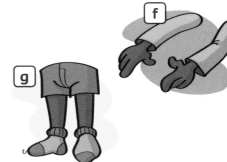

f

g

h

i

j

3 **Listen and number.**

a   **1**

b

c

d

4 **Choose and write. Then colour.**

> red   ~~blue~~   yellow   green   black   white
> pink   purple   brown   orange

1 I've got a _blue_ head
and a _____ face.

2 I've got a _____ tummy,
_____ arms and
_____ hands.

3 I've got _____ legs,
_____ knees and
_____ feet.

I'm an action figure.
My name's _____.

1 [After you read] **Remember the story. Look and number.**

2 [Values] **Look and tick (✔) or cross (✗).**

3 💡 **Look and colour.**

1 **Look, trace and number.**

☐ stretch

 **1**  **2**  **3**

☐ clap

1 move

4  **5**  **6**

☐ bend

☐ touch

☐ stamp

2 **Read and match.**

1 move	your legs	**a** 	**b** 
2 stretch	your hands		
3 touch	your feet	**c** 	**d** 
4 clap	your arms		
5 stamp	your knees	**e** 	**f** 
6 bend	your toes		

»» Extra practice, page 36

1 **Read and tick (✔) or cross (✗).**

1 I've got ten fingers.

2 I've got four arms.

3 I've got three legs.

4 I've got seven toes.

2 **Choose, draw and write.**

> one   two   ten

> head   ~~face~~   tummy
> arms   hands   fingers
> legs   knees   feet   toes

1 I've got _____one face_____.

2 I've got _____.

3 I've got _____.

4 I've got _____.

My name's _____.

1 **Look and colour.**

1 2 3 4 5 6 7 8 9 10

yellow   red   purple   pink   brown   blue   green   black   orange   white

2 After you read **Read and write** Yes **or** No.

1 My name's Sally.   _Yes_

2 I like Chinese New Year at school.   _____

3 It's a Chinese dinosaur.   _____

4 I've got the head. It's purple.   _____

5 I walk and stamp my feet.   _____

6 My friends walk and bend their knees.   _____

English in action
Paying a compliment

1 **Write, draw and colour. Then act out.**

robot   action figure   dragon   cat   teddy   dinosaur

head   tummy   face   body

Look at my picture.

It's a _____ costume.

Yes. Look at the _____. It's big.

Wow! What a cool _____.

Thank you.

My _____
costume

Phonics

2 (3.18) **Listen, write and match.**

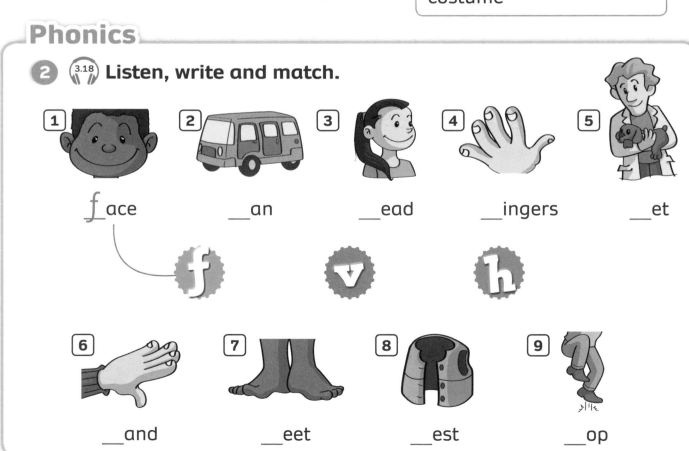

1 _f_ace

2 __an

3 __ead

4 __ingers

5 __et

f   v   h

6 __and

7 __eet

8 __est

9 __op

1 **Read and number.**

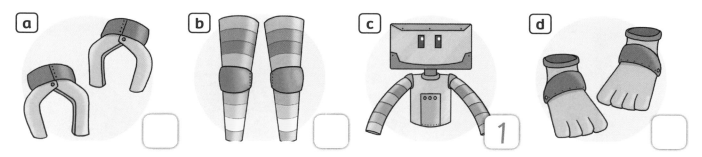

a   b   c   **1**   d

1 I've got one head and two arms.

2 I've got two hands and four fingers.

3 I've got two knees and two legs.

4 I've got two feet and eight toes.

2 **Look and write.**

~~body~~ toes hands feet

1 Move your ___body___ .

2 Stamp your _____ .

3 Clap your _____ .

4 Touch your _____ .

 1

 2

 3

 4

3 **Draw and write.**

I've got _____ and _____ .

Picture dictionary, page 113

1 **Read and number.**

☐ I've got one face, one hand and two big feet.

1 I've got two heads, four arms and three legs.

☐ I've got one body, three knees and three feet.

☐ I've got six arms, six hands and two legs.

2 ✱ **Make up an exercise routine for a friend. Draw and act out.**

~~bend~~ stamp clap stretch move touch

1 _Bend_ your knees.

2 _____ your legs.

3 _____ your toes.

4 _____ your feet.

1

2

3

4

Get ready for...

Pre A1 Starters Listening Part 3

1 🎯 🎧 3.21 **Listen and tick (✔) the box.**

1 Which action figure is it?

A ☐   B ✔   C ☐

2 Which doll is it?

A ☐   B ☐   C ☐

3 Which robot is it?

A ☐   B ☐   C ☐

4 Which teddy is it?

A ☐   B ☐   C ☐

1 **Look and write.**

> alien   book   helicopter   computer   ~~monster~~   robot

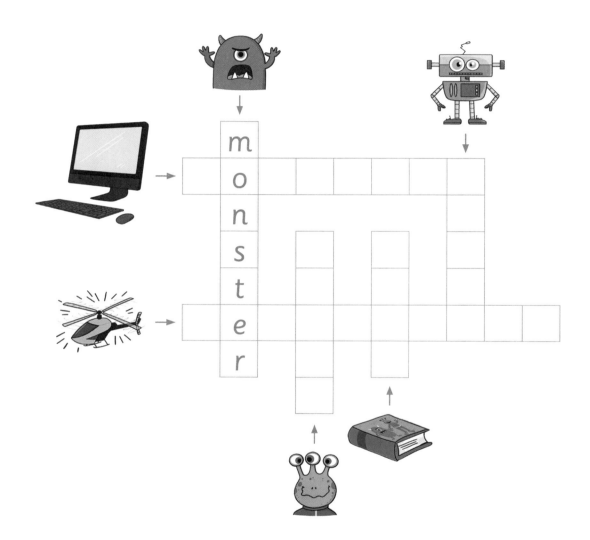

2 **Look at Activity 1. Read and match.**

1 Look at the alien. Is it funny?

2 Look at the monster. Is it funny?

3 Look at the helicopter. Is it noisy?

a Yes, it is.

b Yes, it is.

c No, it isn't.

3 Draw three toys. Then write and circle.

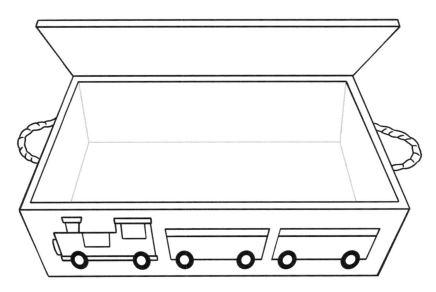

1 Look at my _____.   It's funny scary great .

2 Look at my _____.   It's cool great fantastic .

3 Look at my _____.   It's funny noisy cool .

4 Read and order the dialogue.

[ ]   My favourite book is Cinderella. It's fantastic!

[ ]   Hansel and Gretel. It's scary. What's yours?

[1] What's your favourite book?

5 Read and write. Use different **books** and **adjectives**.

What's your favourite book?

_____. It's _____. What's yours?

My favourite book is _____. It's _____!

4 Meet my family

1 ⏱ **Look at Pupil's Book page 44. Read and write.**

two   brown   ~~Ben and Sam~~

1 Where's Lucy?   With _____Ben and Sam_____.

2 How many balls can you see?   _____

3 What colour is the big bag?   It's _____.

2 **Look, write and match.**

me   granny   mum   dad   aunt   uncle
brother   sister   cousin   grandad

_____me_____

3 **Listen and number.**

4 **Look and match.**

This is my brother.

This is my granny.

This is my mum.

This is my uncle.

1 `After you read` **Remember the story. Read, write and match.**

mum ~~baby~~ cousin dad uncle

1 It's my ___baby___ cousin.

2 This is my _____ and _____.

3 This is my _____, Andy.

4 Oh! It's my _____!

2 `Values` **Draw and write.**

granny
grandad   mother
father   aunt   uncle
sister   brother   me
cousin

This is me and my
_____.

3 **Look and colour.**

Vocabulary and Grammar ④

1 **Find, circle and write.**

b	c	e	a	r	o	m	l
t	s	b	v	h	a	i	r
n	o	s	e	m	g	h	l
o	m	o	u	t	h	p	r
f	l	g	e	y	e	m	h

1 _eye_

5 _____

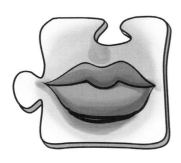

2 _____

3 _____

4 _____

2 **Read and tick (✔).**

1 This is my   sister   ✔   brother   ☐ .

2 She's got a   big   ☐   small   ☐   mouth.

3 She's got   red   ☐   black   ☐   hair.

4 She's got   green   ☐   blue   ☐   eyes.

»» Extra practice, page 48

1 **Read and tick (✔).**

This is my sister, Ana.

She's got black hair.

She's got a big mouth.

She's got blue eyes.

She's got a small nose.

She's got big ears.

2 **Choose and draw. Then circle and write.**

mum   dad   brother
sister   grandad   granny
uncle   aunt   cousin

Who's this?

It's my _____.

His Her name's _____.

He's got She's got _____ hair
and _____ eyes.

He's got She's got a _____ nose.

CULTURE 4

1 **Read and match.**

cake

picture

grey hair

a happy smile

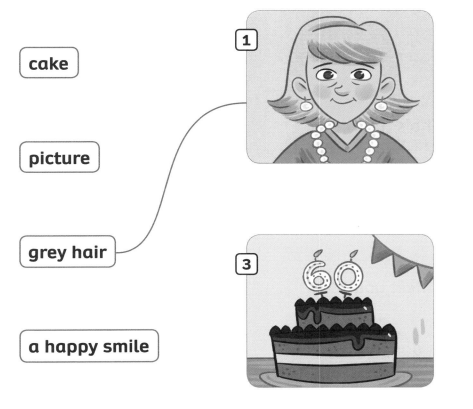

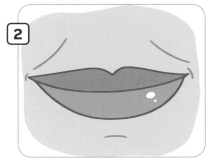

2 After you read **Read and circle.**

1 My name's (Kim) Marie .

2 It's my grandad's granny's birthday today.

3 He's 6 60 today.

4 He's got grey blond hair.

5 He's got a happy brother smile .

English in action
Introducing family and friends

1 **Write, draw and colour. Then act out.**

granny   sister   friend   mum   dad

Hi, _____. Who's this?

Hi, _____. This is my _____.

His Her name's _____.

Hello, _____. Nice to meet you.

Hello, _____. Nice to meet you, too.

My _____

Phonics

2 (4.18) **Listen, write and match.**

1 m͟um

2 __est

3 __even

4 __oo

m   n   s   z

5 __e

6 __ew

7 __ister

8 __ip

1 **Look and write.**

granny   brother   ~~mum~~   sister

1  It's my ___mum___ .   **2** It's my _____.

3 It's _____.   **4** It's _____.

2 **Read, write and colour.**

He's got   She's got   ~~cousin~~   aunt   uncle

1 This is my
___cousin___. ___He's___
___got___ red hair
and blue eyes.

2 This is my
_____. _____
_____ blond hair
and brown eyes.

3 This is my
_____. _____
_____ black hair
and green eyes.

3 ☀ **Read, write and draw.**

This is my _____.

_____ got _____ hair.

_____ got _____ eyes.

1 **Read, find and write.**

Who's this?

mum	dad	brother	sister	granny
grandad	aunt	uncle	cousin	baby cousin

1 She's got brown hair and big eyes. It's my _____mum_____.

2 He's got big, blue eyes and a small mouth. It's my _____.

3 She's got small, brown eyes and no hair. It's my _____.

4 He's got green eyes and a big nose. It's my _____.

5 She's got red hair and a small mouth. It's my _____.

6 He's got small eyes and a big mouth. It's my _____.

Pre A1 Starters Listening Part 4

1   **Listen and colour.**

5 Help the animals!

1 ⏱ **Look at Pupil's Book page 54. Read and write.**

purple   Einstein   one

1 What colour is the car?   It's _____ purple _____.

2 How many bikes can you see?   _____

3 He's got four legs. Who is it?   It's _____.

2 **Look, write and match. Then colour.**

~~dog~~   parrot   tortoise   snake   guinea pig
mouse   cat   fish   spider   rabbit

___ dog ___

1   2   3

_____

_____   _____

4   5   6

_____   _____

8

_____   9   10

7   _____

3 (5.5) **Listen and tick (✔).**

1 a   b ✔ ☐

2 a   b ☐ ☐

3 a   b ☐ ☐

4 a   b ☐ ☐

4 **Look, match and write.**

cats ~~fish~~ mice spiders

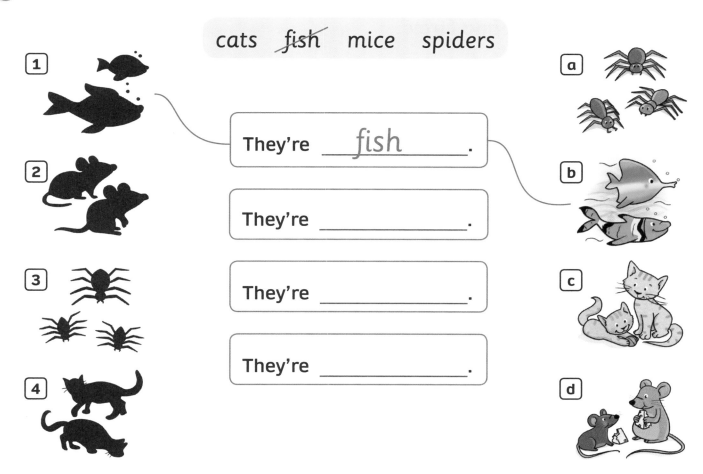

1   They're _____fish_____.

2   They're _____.

3   They're _____.

4   They're _____.

a

b

c

d

1 After you read **Remember the story. Read, write and number.**

guinea pigs   mice   ~~animals~~   eggs

They're _____ .

Let's help the __animals__ .

These are _____ .

They're white _____ .

2 ✓ Values **Look and circle.**

1	2	3	4	5
Yes (No)	Yes No	Yes No	Yes No	Yes No

3 💡 **Look and colour.**

The strange eggs

1 **Look and write.**

tail   fur   shell   wings   teeth   feathers

1 **tail**

2 _____

3 _____

4 _____

5 _____

6 _____

2 **Look, read and circle.**

1 It's got short fur. Is it a cat?   <u>Yes, it is.</u>   No, it isn't.

2 It's got a long tail. Is it a dog?   Yes, it is.   No, it isn't.

3 It's got a big shell. Is it a tortoise?   Yes, it is.   No, it isn't.

4 It's got feathers and two wings. Is it a parrot?   Yes, it is.   No, it isn't.

5 It's got small teeth. Is it a rabbit?   Yes, it is.   No, it isn't.

1 **Read and match.**

1 What are these? They're guinea pigs.

2 What are these? They're fish.

3 What are these? They're spiders.

4 It's got big teeth. It's a rabbit.

5 It's got a short tail. It's a tortoise.

6 It's got long feathers. It's a parrot.

2 **Choose, draw and write.**

mice   snakes   tortoises   fish   guinea pigs   parrots

What are these?

They're _____.

CULTURE

1 **Read, circle and colour.**

prize   show

prize   show

2 **After you read** **Read and write** Yes **or** No.

1 My name's Millie.   _Yes_

2 I'm from the UK.   _____

3 This is my pet – my cat, Rollo.   _____

4 I'm at a dog show in my school.   _____

5 Look! This dog has got a prize.   _____

6 You can see a lot of robots at this show. _____

English in action
Asking about pets

1 **Write, draw and colour. Then act out.**

parrot   mouse   tortoise   snake

What kind of pet have you got?

I've got a _____. What about you?

I've got a _____.

My _____

Phonics

2 (5.18) **Listen, write and match.**

1 sOcks

2 l__gs

3 sh__ll

4 d__g

5 r__d

6 d__ll

7 p__n

8 m__p

1 Look and write.

They're   It's

1 What are these? _They're_ cats.

2 What's this? _____ a guinea pig.

3 What are these? _____ snakes.

4 What's this? _____ a mouse.

2 Look and circle.

1 It's big small .
It's got a long short tail.
It's got feathers fur .

2 It's big small .
It's got a tail teeth .
It's got a shell wings .

3 Read, write and draw.

I've got a pet!

It's big small .

It's got _____

and _____ .

It's a _____ .

1 **Count and write.**

> fish   cats   spiders   guinea pigs   rabbits
> mice   snakes   dogs   parrot   tortoises

nine ___fish___

six _____

four _____

seven _____

ten _____

three _____

two _____

one _____

five _____

eight _____

2 **Read and match.**

1    2    3

a It's got a long tail.
It's small.
It's got a big nose.
It's got black and
white fur.

b It's got a short tail.
It's got four long
legs.
It's got a small nose.
It's got brown fur.

c It's long.
It's got a short tail.
It's got short legs.
It's got big teeth.
It's brown.

Get ready for...

Pre A1 Starters Reading and Writing Part 2

1 🎯 **Look and read. Write Yes or No.**

1 The tortoise is under the table.   _No_

2 The mouse is small.   _____

3 The parrot is red and blue.   _____

4 The snake is long.   _____

5 The dog is big.   _____

6 Do you like peas?

1 ⏱ **Look at Pupil's Book page 64. Read and write.**

> rabbit ~~two~~ on

1 How many dogs can you see? _____ two _____

2 Find an animal with big ears. _____

3 Where are the apples? They're _____ the table.

2 **Look, write and match. Then colour.**

> apple   orange   banana   tomato   carrot
> potato   beans   peas   ~~rice~~   pasta

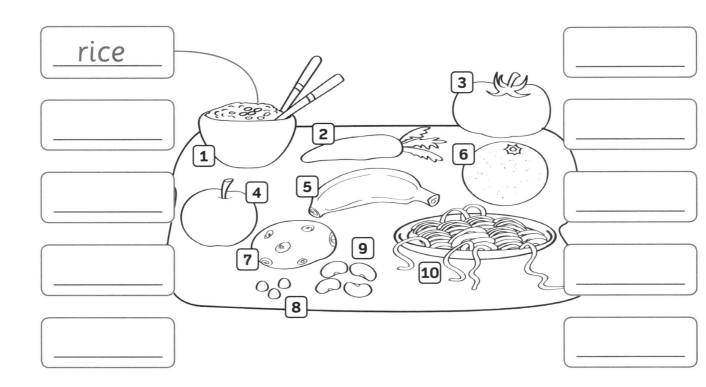

rice

3 6.5 **Listen and number.**

a

☐

b

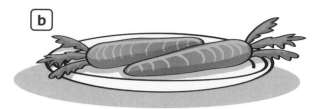

☐

c

1

d

☐

4 **Make sentences true for you. Then match.**

like   don't like

1 I ___like___ bananas.

a

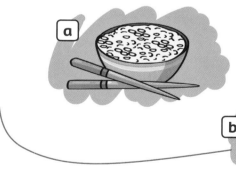

b

2 I _____ apples.

3 I _____ rice.

c

d

4 I _____ beans.

1 **After you read** **Remember the story. Read, write and match.**

pasta   ~~vegetables~~   bananas   peas   potatoes

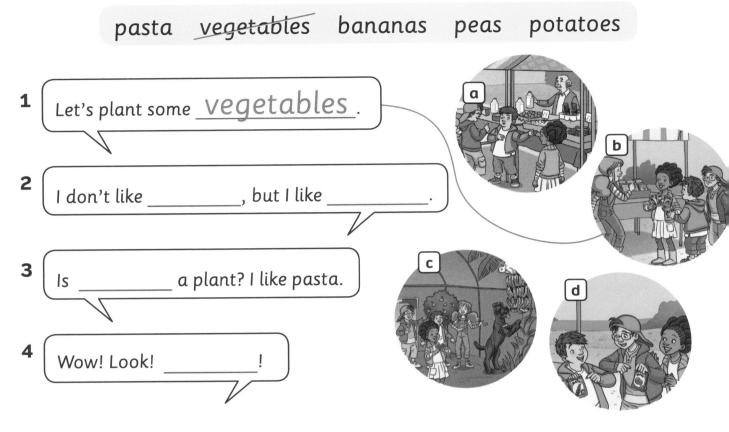

1 Let's plant some ___vegetables___ .

2 I don't like _____, but I like _____.

3 Is _____ a plant? I like pasta.

4 Wow! Look! _____!

2 **Values** **Look and tick (✔) or cross (✗).**

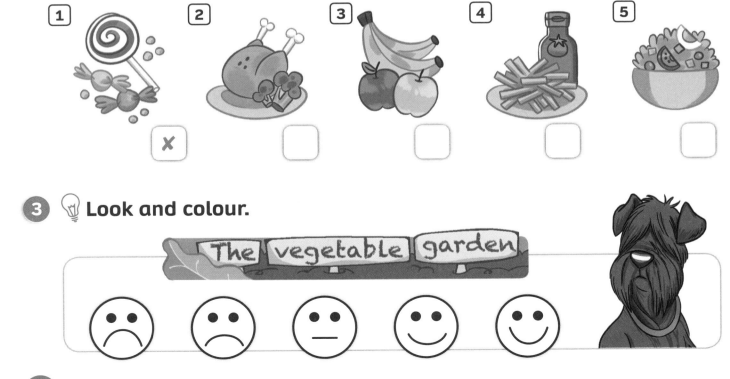

3 **Look and colour.**

The vegetable garden

1 **Match and write.**

1 fi   eese

2 mi   sh

3 eg   lk

4 ch   ce

5 jui   gs

_____

_____

fish

_____

_____

2 **Write and circle. Answer for you.**

chicken   ~~bread~~   meat   water

1 Do you like __bread__ ?

   Yes, I do.   No, I don't.

2 Do you like _____ ?

   Yes, I do.   No, I don't.

3 Do you like _____ ?

   Yes, I do.   No, I don't.

4 Do you like _____ ?

   Yes, I do.   No, I don't.

Extra practice, page 68

1 **Read and tick (✔).**

1 Do you like apples? Yes, I do.

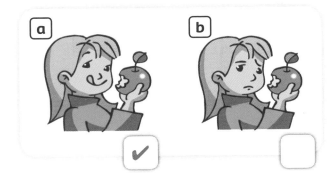

2 Do you like meat? No, I don't.

3 Do you like beans? Yes, I do.

4 Do you like eggs? No, I don't.

2 **Look and write.**

1 Do you like _____*cheese*_____ ? Yes, _____*I do*_____.

2 Do you _____ ? No, _____.

3 Do _____ ? No, _____.

4 _____ ? _____

1 **Read and match.**

fruit chocolate vegetables pancakes

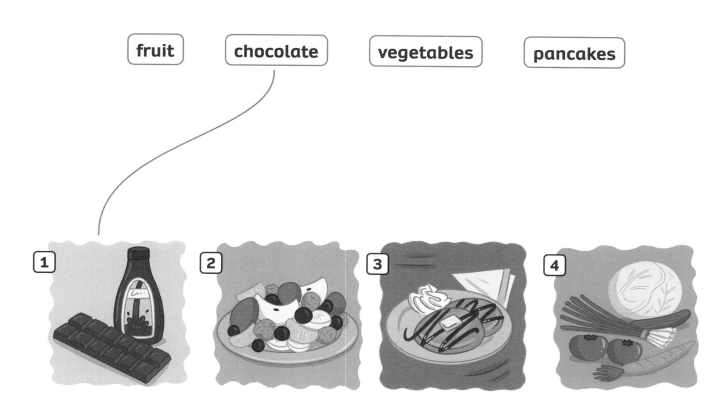

1   2   3   4

2 **After you read** **Read and circle.**

1 People like pancakes chocolate
   in lots of different countries.

2 I like pancakes from Japan with
   meat eggs and vegetables.

3 I like pancakes from Russia with
   fruit vegetables .

4 I like pancakes from France with
   chocolate fruit .

5 I like them with cheese and
   fruit vegetables too.

English in action
Asking for food and drink

1 **Write, draw and colour. Then act out.**

| an orange | a banana | a carrot | juice | water |

I'm hungry. Can I have _____, please?

Yes, sure. What about a drink?

Yes, please. Can I have some _____, please?

Here you are.

Thank you.

My food and drink

Phonics

2 (6.18) **Listen, write and match.**

| 1 | 2 | 3 | 4 | 5 |

_C_ at   __arden   __am   __ar   __uinea pig

c   **g**   **j**

| 6 | 7 | 8 | 9 |

__oy   __old   __oal   __uice

1 Look and write.

juice   rice   ~~eggs~~   pasta

1 I like _____ *eggs* _____.

2 I don't like _____.

3 _____

4 _____

2 Look and write. Then circle.

~~carrots~~   oranges   fish   bread

1 Do you like ___ carrots ___?   ☺ (Yes, I do.) No, I don't.

2 Do you _____?   ☹ Yes, I do.   No, I don't.

3 Do _____?   ☺ Yes, I do.   No, I don't.

4 _____?   ☹ Yes, I do.   No, I don't.

3 Look, choose and write.

Menu
Rice ----
Pasta --
Chicken ---
Water ---

Can I have _____ and _____, please?

Yes, sure. What about a drink?

Yes, please. _____

Here you are.

_____

1 **Make a wordsearch for a friend.**

a	b	r	e	a	d	x

 ✔

2 **Order and answer for you.**

1 fish / you / like / Do _____? _____

2 eggs / like / you / Do _____? _____

3 you / juice / like / Do _____? _____

Get ready for...

1   **Listen and write the answers.**

1 Do you like chicken, Sue? _____No, I don't._____

2 Do you like rice, Nick? _____

3 Do you like bananas, Eve? _____

4 What do you like, Anna? I like _____ and _____.

5 Do you like cheese, Sam? _____

Language booster 2

1 **Look and write.**

old   young   tall   ~~short~~   beautiful   ugly   small   big

Anna

short

2 **Read and write** he, she **or** it. **Then match.**

1 Look at the man. Is ___he___ young?   **a** Yes, it is.

2 Look at the rabbit. Is _____ big?   **b** No, she isn't.

3 Look at Anna. Is _____ tall?   **c** Yes, he is.

4 Look at the fish. Is _____ ugly?   **d** No, it isn't.

5 Look at the boy. Is _____ young?   **e** No, he isn't.

3 **Read and order the dialogue.**

[ ] Yes, I do. I like rabbits a lot.

[ ] No, not really!

[ ] Cool! I really like guinea pigs, too.

[1] Look at this beautiful rabbit! Do you like rabbits?

[ ] So do I. Do you like spiders?

4 **Read and write. Use different animals.**

Look at this beautiful _____!
Do you like _____?

Yes, I do. I like _____ a lot.

Cool! I really like _____, too.

So do I. Do you like _____?

No, not really!

5 **Read and match.**

I'm tall and I've got long brown hair. I like rabbits and guinea pigs. I don't like snakes or spiders.

[a] [b] [c]

7 It's windy!

1 ⏱ **Look at Pupil's Book page 78. Read and write.**

purple   three   ~~mouse~~   ~~cat~~

1 What pets can you see?   _A mouse_ and _a cat_ .

2 What colour is the slide?   It's _____.

3 How many cars can you see? _____

2 **Look and write.**

sunny   cloudy   ~~rainy~~   windy   foggy
stormy   snowy   hot   cold

1 _rainy_   **2** _____   **3** _____   **4** _____   **5** _____

6 _____   **7** _____   **8** _____   **9** _____

3 🎧 7.5 **Listen and tick (✔) or cross (✗).**

4 **Look and write.**

> foggy ~~rainy~~ windy stormy
> ~~sunny~~ snowy cloudy cold

1 It's _____rainy_____.

It isn't _____sunny_____.

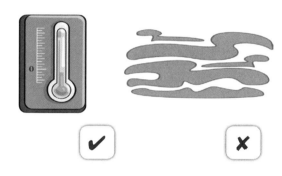

2 It's _____.

It isn't _____.

3 It's _____.

It isn't _____.

4 It's _____.

It isn't _____.

1 After you read **Remember the story. Read and write** True **or** False.

1 It's hot and sunny now. ___True___

2 It's hot. Brr! I'm wearing shorts! _____

3 The weather is crazy today! _____

4 Oh no! It's foggy. _____

2 Values **Look and tick (✔) or cross (✗).**

3 💡 **Look and colour.**

1 **Look, write and match.**

boots   trousers   skirt   shorts   shoes   ~~T-shirt~~   sweater   coat

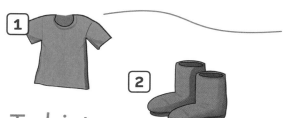

1 T-shirt

2 _____

It's sunny and hot.

5 _____

6 _____

3 _____

4 _____

It's cold and snowy.

7 _____

8 _____

2 **Look and write.**

a sweater   a coat   shorts   a skirt
trousers   boots   a T-shirt   shoes

 **1**

 **2**

 **3**

 **4**

1 I'm wearing __a T-shirt__ , __shorts__ and __shoes__ .

2 I'm wearing _____ , _____ and _____ .

3 I'm wearing _____ , _____ and _____ .

4 I'm wearing _____ , _____ and _____ .

»» **Extra practice, page 80**

1 **Read and colour.**

1 I'm wearing a yellow hat, a blue T-shirt and red shorts. It's hot and sunny.

2 I'm wearing a green coat, purple trousers and brown boots. It's cold and snowy.

2 **Draw and write.**

1 It's hot and sunny.
What are you wearing?

I'm wearing _____, _____
and _____.

2 It's cold and snowy.
What are you wearing?

I'm wearing _____, _____
and _____.

1 **Look and write.**

sculpture   sled   fireworks   ~~ice~~   castle

1

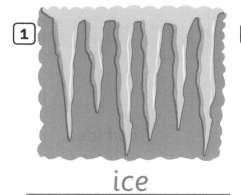

ice

2

_____

3

_____

4

_____

5

_____

2 After you read **Read and tick (✔) or cross (✗).**

1 Harbin is in the UK.   ✗

2 It is famous for an ice and
snow festival.

3 You can see snow pictures.

4 You can ride in a dog sled.

5 At night you can see fireworks.

6 Bring your sweater and boots!
It's snowy and hot!

English in action
Giving instructions

1 **Write, draw and colour. Then act out.**

| hot | rainy | sunny | stormy | hat | coat | boots |

1

Brr. It's _____.

Put on your _____!

Good idea.

It's _____.

2

Phew! It's _____.

Take off your _____!

Good idea.

It's _____.

Phonics

2 (7.18) **Listen, write and match.**

| 1 | 2 | 3 | 4 | 5 |

_a_pple   f__sh   b__d   r__n   h__t

a   e   i   o   u

| 6 | 7 | 8 | 9 | 10 |

__gg   h__t   p__nk   l__ng   d__ck

1 **Look and write.**

foggy   hot   windy   rainy   snowy   stormy   ~~sunny~~   ~~cloudy~~

✔   ✗   ✔   ✗

1 It's _____sunny_____.

It isn't _____cloudy_____.

2 It's _____.

It isn't _____.

✔   ✗   ✔   ✗

3 _____

_____

4 _____

_____

2 **Read, write and draw.**

1 What's the weather like today?

It's _____ and _____.

It isn't _____.

2 What are you wearing today?

I'm wearing _____

_____.

1 **Find and circle.**

skirtshortsshoescoatsweatertrousersT-shirtboots

2 **Look and write. Then find and tick (✔).**

windy

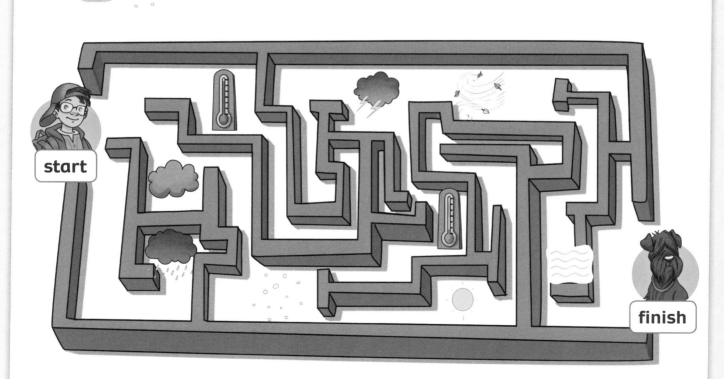

start

finish

Get ready for...

Pre A1 Starters Reading and Writing Part 5

1 🎯 **Look at the pictures and read the questions. Write one-word answers.**

1 What's the weather like? It's _sunny_ .

2 What are you wearing? A green _____ and blue _____ .

3 What's the weather like? It's _____ .

4 What are you wearing? A yellow _____ and brown _____ .

8 Who's at home?

1 ⏱ **Look at Pupil's Book page 88. Read and write.**

bedroom ~~granny~~ blue

1 Who's wearing an orange T-shirt? _____ granny _____

2 What colour is the car? It's _____.

3 Where's the blue chair? In the _____.

2 **Look, write and match.**

attic   bedroom   ~~flat~~   bathroom   house
kitchen   hall   garage   living room   garden

_____ flat _____

1

2

3

4

5

6

7

8

9

10

3 🎧 (8.5) **Listen and number.**

4 **Look and write.**

~~living room~~   bedroom   garden   attic

1 She's in the garden.

<u>She isn't in the garden.</u>
<u>She's in the living room.</u>

2 He's in the bathroom.

_____

_____

3 He's in the kitchen.

_____

_____

4 She's in the garage.

_____

_____

1 After you read **Remember the story. Read and circle.**

1 Where's Lisa?
She's in the
kitchen (bedroom) garden .

2 Where's Ben?
He's in the attic garage hall .

3 Where's she?
She's in the
living room garden house .

4 What's this?
It's a treasure time capsule .

2 Values **Solve the mystery.**

○	●	×	▼	△	◆	⊙	✱	+	■	◈	♣	□
a	c	d	e	g	h	i	m	n	o	r	s	t

○ □ ■ ✱ ⊙ ●   ⊙ ♣   ⊙ +   □ ◆ ▼   △ ○ ◈ × ▼ +

A t o m i c   __ __   __ __   __ __ __   __ __ __ __ __ __

3 💡 **Look and colour.**

The hidden treasure

1 **Look, write and match.**

make lay tidy feed wash clean

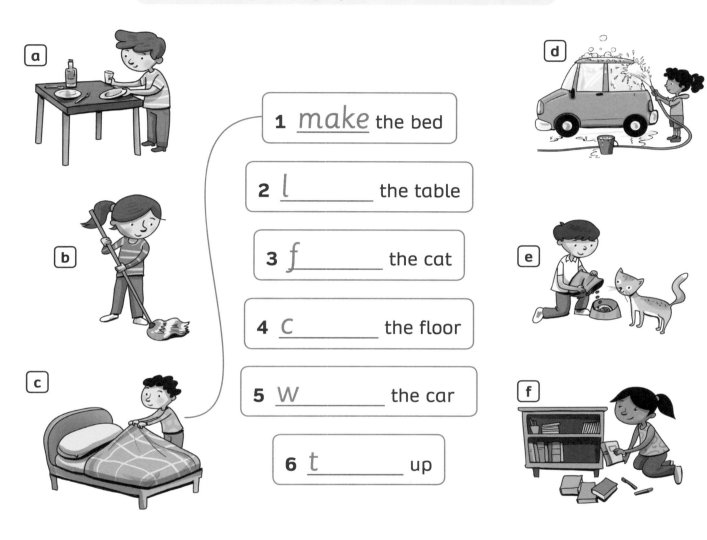

1 __make__ the bed

2 l_____ the table

3 f_____ the cat

4 c_____ the floor

5 w_____ the car

6 t_____ up

2 **Look at Activity 1. Order and write.**

1 making / He's / the / bed ___He's making the bed.___

2 the / laying / table / He's _____

3 He's / the / feeding / cat _____

4 cleaning / She's / floor / the _____

5 car / washing / the / She's _____

6 up / She's / tidying _____

Extra practice, page 90

1 **Read and match.**

1 Where's my dad?
He isn't in the garden.
He's laying the table
in the living room.

2 Where's my sister?
She isn't in the hall.
She's tidying up in
the attic.

3 Where's my mum?
She isn't in the bathroom.
She's making the bed
in the bedroom.

2 **Look and write. Where's Claire?**

the kitchen   the bedroom   feeding the dog

She isn't in _____.

She's _____

in _____.

CULTURE

8

1 **Read and match.**

1

bed

tent

cave

4

2

dining room

5

3

boat

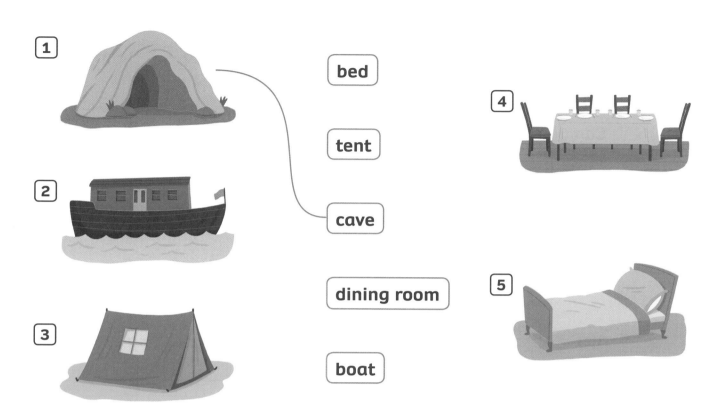

2 After you read **Read and write** Yes **or** No.

1 Is this a bedroom? _____

2 Is he laying the table? _____

3 Is this home in a boat? _____

4 Is the table big? _____

English in action
Asking for and offering to help

1 **Write, draw and colour. Then act out.**

tidy up   feed the cat   wash the car   make the bed   clean the floor

Can you help me, please?

Sure. What can I do?

Can you help me _____?

Yes, of course.

Thank you.

Can you help me _____?

Phonics

2 (8.18) **Listen, write and match.**

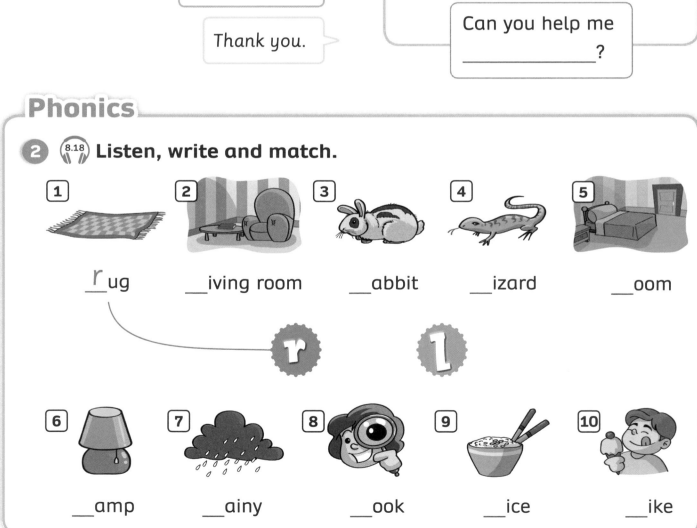

| 1 | 2 | 3 | 4 | 5 |

_r_ug   __iving room   __abbit   __izard   __oom

r   **l**

| 6 | 7 | 8 | 9 | 10 |

__amp   __ainy   __ook   __ice   __ike

1 **Look and write.**

1 ___house___

2 _____

3 _____

4 _____

5 _____

6 _____

7 _____

8 _____

9 _____

10 _____

flat ~~house~~ hall kitchen
living room bedroom bathroom
attic garden garage

2 **Look at Activity 1. Read and write.**

making the bed   laying the table
tidying up   ~~washing the car~~

1 Where's my mum?

She isn't in the bathroom.
She's in the garage.
She's washing the car.

2 Where's my dad?

_____

_____

_____

3 Where's my sister?

_____

_____

_____

4 Where's my brother?

_____

_____

_____

1 **Follow and write.**

bedroom   bathroom   living room   ~~kitchen~~

1 She's in the ___kitchen___ .

2 He's in the _____ .

3 _____

4 _____

2 **Look and write.**

feeding the cat   cleaning the floor
tidying up   ~~making the bed~~

1 She's in the bedroom.
She's making the bed.

2 _____
_____

3 _____
_____

4 _____
_____

Pre A1 Starters Listening Part 1

1 🎯 🎧 (8.20) **Listen and draw lines.**

Jamal

Laura

Jane

Sally

9 Let's play outside

1 ⏱ **Look at Pupil's Book page 98. Read and write.**

pink ~~windy~~ two

1 What's the weather like? It's ___windy___.

2 What colour is Sam's ball? It's _____.

3 How many bikes can you see? _____

2 **Find and circle.**

q	r	c	l	i	m	b	e
w	a	l	k	i	m	s	f
s	k	i	p	r	i	d	e
j	u	m	p	e	r	u	n
b	a	s	p	l	a	y	l
f	l	y	t	n	a	l	s
t	s	w	i	m	o	d	e

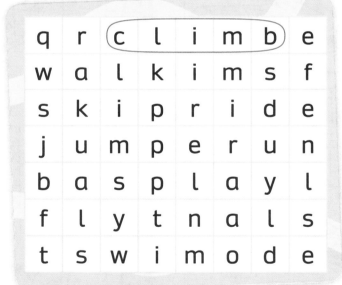

3 🎧 9.5 **Listen and tick (✔) or cross (✗).**

4 **Look and write.**

| can | can't | fly a kite | ~~play football~~ | ride a bike | skip |

1 I __can play football__ .

2 I _____.

3 I _____.

4 I _____.

1 **After you read** Remember the story. Read, circle and match.

1 Can you (swim) jump , Ben?

2 No, let's climb walk to the island.

3 Oh, no! Atomic can't swim skip .

4 Now I can fly my kite ride my bike .

2 **Values** Look and write Yes or No.

Yes ___ ___ ___ ___

3 Look and colour.

Hooray for Einstein

1 **Look and number.**

☐ dance   ☐ draw   ☐ sing

☐ play the guitar   ☐ take photos   ☐ 1 paint

2 **Look at Activity 1. Write and circle.**

> play the guitar   paint   take photos

1 Can you _____?   Yes, I can.   No, I can't.

2 Can you _____?   Yes, I can.   No, I can't.

3 Can you _____?   Yes, I can.   No, I can't.

》》 Extra practice, page 96

1 **Read and circle. Circle in green what Anna can do and in red what she can't do.**

Hi, I'm Anna.
What can I do?
I can ride a bike
and I can swim.
I can play football,
but I can't play baseball.
I can't climb,
but I can fly a kite.

2 **Look and write.**

I can   I can't   take photos   skip   climb   play baseball

1 Can you __skip__, Robert?

Yes, _____.

But _____

_____.

2 Can you _____, Betty?

No, _____.

But _____

_____.

1 **Read and tick (✔).**

1 cowboy

2 horse

3 campfire

4 picnic

2 | After you read | **Read and write.**

Yes, I can.   No, I can't.

1 You can go to a dude ranch in the UK.   _No, I can't._

2 You can ride trains here.   _____

3 You can eat inside at a table.   _____

4 You can have a picnic under the trees.   _____

5 You can play football by a campfire.   _____

6 You can sing songs by a campfire.   _____

English in action
Making plans

1 **Write, draw and colour. Then act out.**

park   playground   play baseball   take photos   walk   run

It's sunny!

Let's go to the _____.

OK. We can _____.

Good idea. Let's ask Dad.

Let's go to the _____.

Phonics

2 **Listen, write and match.**

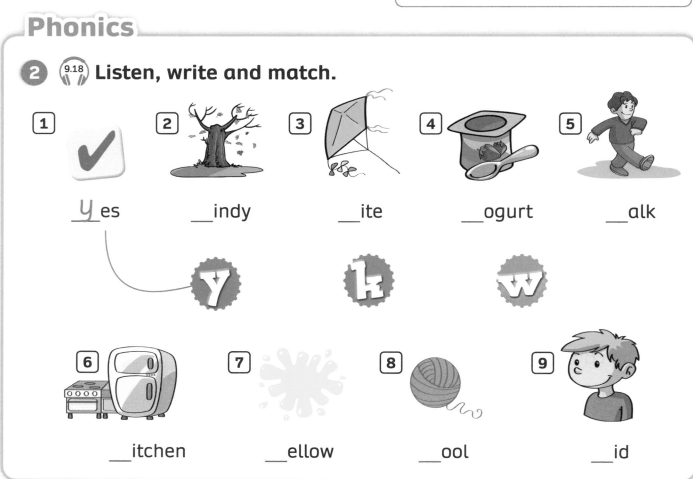

1 ✔ _Y_ es   2 __indy   3 __ite   4 __ogurt   5 __alk

6 __itchen   7 __ellow   8 __ool   9 __id

1 **Order and draw.**

1 a bike / can't / I / ride

I can't ride a bike.

2 play / can / football / I

_____

3 climb / can / I / a tree

_____

4 I / swim / can't / in the sea

_____

2 **Look, write and answer for you.**

Yes, I can.   No, I can't.

 play the guitar   dance   paint   draw

1 Can you ___play the guitar___?

Yes, I can. _____

2 Can you _____?

_____

3 _____?

_____

4 _____?

_____

Picture dictionary, page 119

1 **Look, read and number.**

a I can sing, ride a bike and fly a kite.

b I can't paint, but I can dance and play baseball. `1`

c I can't draw, but I can play the guitar and run.

d I can play football, jump and take photos.

2 **Write and draw.**

I can _____,
_____
and _____.

I can't _____,
but I can _____
and _____.

Get ready for...

Pre A1 Starters Reading and Writing Part 1

1 🎯 **Look and read. Put a tick (✔) or a cross (✗) in the box.**

1
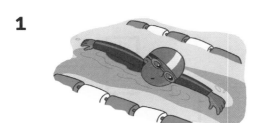
I can swim.
 ✔

2

I can't ride a bike.

3

I can skip.

4

I can't paint.

5

I can't run.

Language booster 3

1 **Find and number in order.**

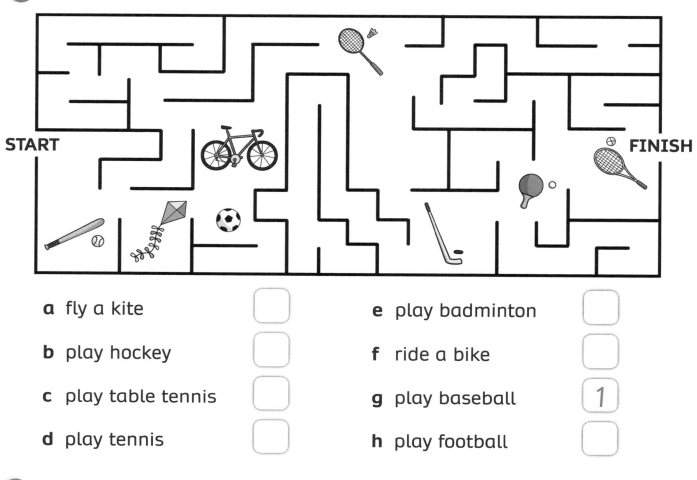

START   FINISH

a fly a kite ☐   **e** play badminton ☐

b play hockey ☐   **f** ride a bike ☐

c play table tennis ☐   **g** play baseball 1

d play tennis ☐   **h** play football ☐

2 **Look at Activity 1. Circle the activities you enjoy.**

3 **Draw and write activities for you.**

1 I enjoy _____.   **2** I don't enjoy _____.

4 **Read and order the dialogue.**

[ ] What about hockey?

[1] What shall we do today?

[ ] No, thanks. I don't enjoy baseball.

[ ] Good idea. I like hockey. It's fun!

[ ] Let's play baseball.

5 **Read and write. Use different activities.**

What shall we do today?

Let's play _____.

No, thanks. I don't enjoy _____.

What about _____?

Good idea. I like _____. It's fun!

6 **What does Dan enjoy? Read and tick (✔) or cross (✗).**

I'm Dan. I enjoy table tennis. It's fun. I enjoy badminton and tennis, too. I enjoy football. I don't enjoy baseball or hockey.

a [ ]

b [ ]

c [ ]

d [✔]

e [ ]

f [ ]

Bonfire Night

1 **Trace, match and colour.**

fireworks

November

sparkler

rocket

night

bonfire

moon

gloves

1 black **2** brown **3** white

4 orange **5** red **6** green **7** blue

8 yellow **9** pink **10** purple

2 **Read and match.**

a

b

c

d

e

f

g

h

1 I see fireworks.

2 I see the moon.

3 I see a bonfire.

4 I've got a sparkler.

5 I've got gloves.

6 It's a rocket.

7 It's November.

8 It's night.

3 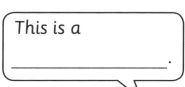 **Draw a firework. Then write.**

This is a

_____.

Earth Day

1 **Trace and match.**

recycle

pick up   plant   rubbish

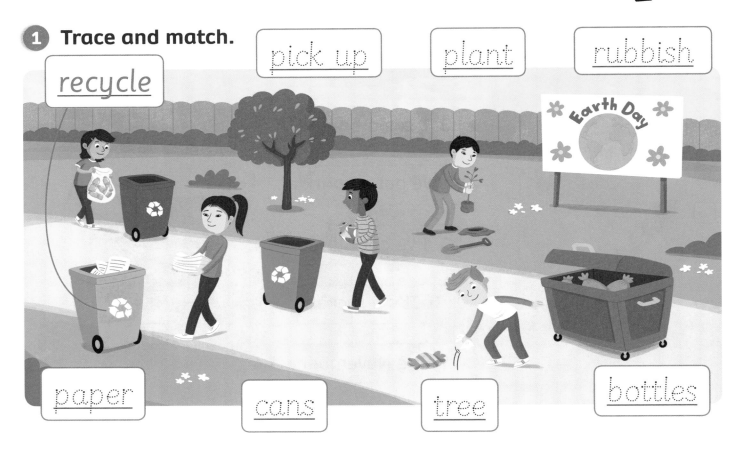

paper   cans   tree   bottles

2 **Find, count and write.**

trees ☐

bottles ☐

cans ☐

3 Trace and match.

1 I recycle _bottles_.

2 I pick up _rubbish_.

3 I recycle _cans_.

4 I plant a _tree_.

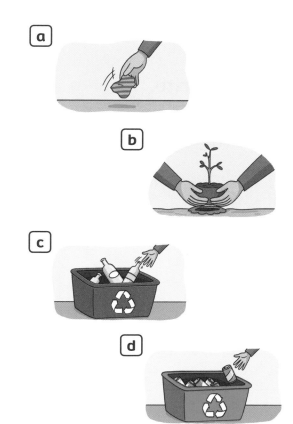

a
b
c
d

4 What is in your recycle bin? Draw and write.

I like Earth Day. I recycle _____.

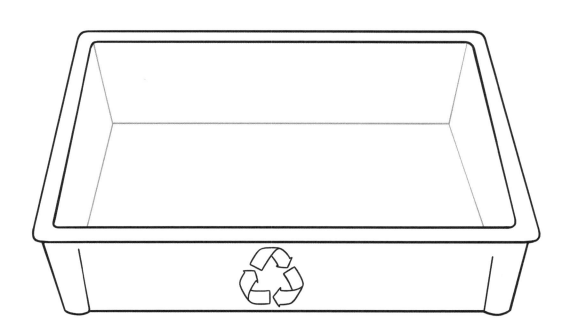

Kite Festival Day

1 **Look and write.**

string   kite   horse   teddy   ~~sky~~   bird   fish   tail

1 ___sky___
2 _____
3 _____
4 _____
5 _____
6 _____
7 _____
8 _____

2 **Find and colour.**

1 ● red
2 ● green
3 ○ white
4 ● brown
5 ● blue
6 ● yellow
7 ● orange
8 ● pink
9 ● black
10 ● purple

3 **Read and write. Then match.**

spring   teddy   ~~windy~~   tail   kite

1 It's __windy__.

2 It's S_____.

3 I've got a purple k_____.

4 Look at the long t_____ on my kite!

5 Do you like my t_____ kite?

a

b   Yes, I do.

c

d

e

4 **Draw a kite. Then write.**

My kite is a _____.

Picture dictionary

 one

 red

 two

 yellow

 three

 blue

 four

 green

 five

 black

 six

 purple

 seven

 orange

 eight

 brown

 nine

 pink

 ten

 white

 car

 teddy

 plane

 dinosaur

 puzzle

 slide

 yoyo

 bike

 building set

 scooter

 doll

 kite

 action figure

 ball

 robot

 swing

 bag

 rubber

 book

 scissors

 pencil case

 shelf

 pen

 computer

 pencil

 cupboard

 crayon

 desk

 ruler

 chair

 sharpener

 table

 head

 face

 tummy

 arms

 hands

 fingers

 legs

 knees

 feet

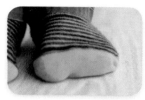 toes

 move

 bend

 strech

 touch

 stamp

 clap

blond   me   hair   granny   mouth   mum
cousin   eyes   aunt   brother   ears   dad   nose
sister   brown   uncle   red   black   grandad

feathers   small   shell   long   cat   short   dog
wings   rabbit   guineapig   teeth   snake   mouse
parrot   fur   tortoise   big   fish   tail   spider

_____

_____

_____

_____

_____

_____

_____

_____

_____

_____

_____

_____

_____

_____

_____

_____

_____

_____

_____

_____

juice   fish   eggs   bread   pasta   apple   water
tomato   rice   milk   chicken   cheese   banana
meat   carrot   potato   beans   orange   peas

_____   _____

_____   _____

_____   _____

_____   _____

_____   _____

_____   _____

_____   _____

_____   _____

_____   _____

_____

T-shirt   foggy   skirt   boots   snowy   hot
trousers   windy   shoes   stormy   coat   cold
rainy   cloudy   sweater   shorts   sunny

_____

_____

_____

_____

_____

_____

_____

_____

_____

_____

_____

_____

_____

_____

_____

_____

_____

clean the floor   flat   lay the table   living room   tidy up
kitchen   attic   wash the car   house   bathroom   garden
make the bed   bedroom   hall   feed the cat   garage

_____

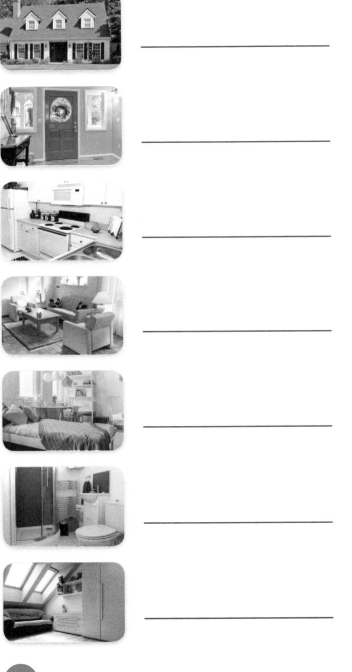

_____

_____

_____

_____

_____

_____

_____

_____

_____

play the guitar   climb   take photos   swim   draw
jump   ride a bike   walk   sing   fly a kite   skip
paint   play football   dance   play baseball   run

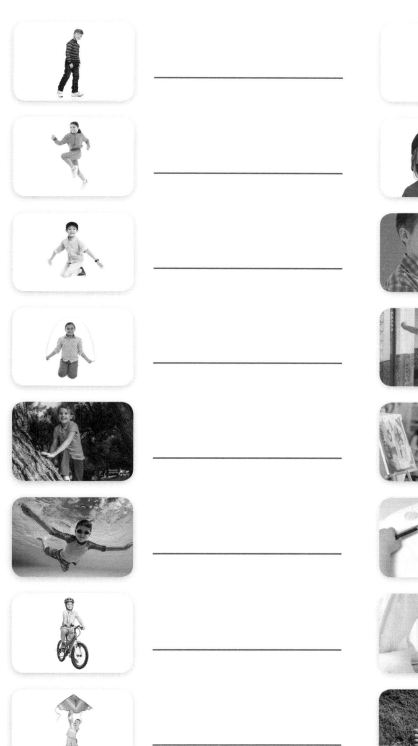

_____

_____

_____

_____

_____

_____

_____

_____

Bonfire Night, Earth Day and Kite Festival Day

rocket   horse   tree   night   bird   tail   recycle
November   rubbish   plant   pick up   gloves   sky
teddy   sparkler   cans   moon   kite   paper
fireworks   bottles   fish   bonfire   string

_____

_____

_____

_____

_____

_____

_____

_____

_____

_____

_____

_____

_____

_____

_____

_____

_____

_____

_____

_____

_____

_____